Heiress

Heiress

Elisabeth Murawski

TEXAS REVIEW PRESS • HUNTSVILLE, TEXAS

Requests for permission to acknowledge material from the work should be sent to:
   Permissions
   Texas Review Press
   English Department
   Sam Houston State University
   Huntsville, TX 77341-2146

LIBRARY OF CONGRESS CATALOGING-IN-PUBLICATION DATA

Names: Murawski, Elisabeth, 1936– author.
Title: Heiress / by Elisabeth Murawski.
Description: First edition. | Huntsville, Texas : Texas Review Press, [2018] |
Stains: the wrong house—Patrimony—Josie—Chicago morning—Child with reader—
   Childish things—Net—The present—Quel dommage —Specs—Heiress—The exchange—
   Position of strength—Thoughts of a potato lover—Regrets—Damages—In changing
   light—Anna and Helen—Tense—Dies Illa—Teneo—Elegiac—Mary, Mary—Old—The
   return—Rachel—Day 5—Stage IV on the coma scale—Lamentation of Christ: sold off to
   pay debts—Still life with Timex—In the meadow—World on East 84th—The Improvi-
   sation—Merrily, merrily—Children of another century—On a fragment from Sappho—
   Again—Spent—Sketch: fade to black—Steep—White, a sequel—Evolution—Bonsai
   lovers—Cumberland—Unrequited—At the pavilion—Before the snow—Willow—
   Waking alone on Sunday morning—Tremor—Tombs—The cardboard shirt—Black
   messengers—In Padua, St. Anthony's Tomb—Rowhouse angel—I underestimate what she
   meant to him—Hopkins Room, University College, Dublin—Eutychus propped on a
   windowsill listens to Paul—Sara's song—Unlike anybody else in the world—Poem on a
   line from a Sufi prayer—Shenandoah scene—For Edward Thomas—Iconic photo:
   Lee Miller in Munich, April, 1945—Musings—Concerto—At the Museum of the Resis-
   tance—A catastrophe of violins—The secret historian—Christ to Kazantzakis—
   Capital—Farther out—Admiral to Isabella. |
Identifiers: LCCN 2018008617 (print) | LCCN 2018010292 (ebook) | ISBN 9781680031690
   (ebook) | ISBN 9781680031683 | ISBN 781680031683¬q(pbk.)
Subjects: LCSH: American poetry—21st century. | LCGFT: Poetry.
Classification: LCC PS3563.U7228 (ebook) | LCC PS3563.U7228 A6 2018 (print) |
   DDC 811/.54—dc23
LC record available at https://lccn.loc.gov/2018008617

Author photo by Janette Ogle
Cover design by Nancy Parsons
Cover image: *Child Wearing a Red Scarf* by Edouard Vuillard, courtesy of the National Gallery
   of Art, Washington, D.C., Ailsa Mellon Bruce Collection

For Walter Cummins

Contents

PART I

Stains: the Wrong House   1

Patrimony   2

Josie   4

Chicago Morning   5

Child with Reader   6

Childish Things   7

Net   8

The Present   9

Quel Dommage   10

Specs   11

Heiress   12

The Exchange   13

Position of Strength   14

Thoughts of a Potato Lover   15

Regrets   16

Damages   17

In Changing Light   18

Anna and Helen   19

Tense   20

Dies Illa   22

Teneo   23

Elegiac   24

Mary, Mary   25

Old   26

PART II

The Return   29

Rachel   30

Day 5   31

Stage IV on the Coma Scale   32

Lamentation of Christ: Sold Off to Pay Debts   33

Still Life with Timex   34

In the Meadow   35

PART III

World on East 84th 39

The Improvisation   40

Merrily, Merrily   41

Children of Another Century   42

On a Fragment from Sappho   43

Again   44

Spent   45

Sketch: Fade to Black   46

Steep   47

White, A Sequel   49

Evolution   51

Bonsai Lovers   52

Cumberland   53

Unrequited   54

At the Pavilion   55

Before the Snow   56

Willow   58

Waking Alone on Sunday Morning   59

PART IV

Tremor   63

Tombs   64

The Cardboard Shirt   65

Black Messengers   66

In Padua: St. Anthony's Tomb   67

Rowhouse Angel   68

I Underestimate What She Meant to Him   69

Hopkins Room, University College, Dublin   70

Eutychus Propped on a Windowsill Listens to Paul   71

Sara's Song   73

Unlike Anybody Else in the World   74

Poem on a Line from a Sufi Prayer   75

Shenandoah Scene   76

For Edward Thomas   77

Iconic Photo: Lee Miller in Munich, April, 1945   78

Musings   79

Concerto   80

At the Museum of the Resistance   81

A Catastrophe of Violins   82

The Secret Historian   83

Christ to Kazantzakis   84

Capital   85

Farther Out   86

Admiral to Isabella   87

Acknowledgments   89

It may be
  that some little root of the sacred tree still lives.
Nourish it then
  that it may leaf and bloom and fill with singing birds.

—BLACK ELK

PART I

Stains: The Wrong House

Here are the yellow walls,
the slick stairs,

the eternal burn ward
with its covered

mirrors, Mrs. P.
hovering on the landing,

acquiescing
in the lie. From then on,

what I saw
walked with a limp:

father, riding bareback,
digging in his heels.

Mother, elegiac,
advertising scars.

I am the mistake.
The pictures go back that far.

The peonies chuckle
in their white peignoirs.

Patrimony

I fit in the crook of his arm
like a watermelon, a sweet
secret. In his dark Sunday suit

he's holding me up
for more than the camera
to see. We're both squinting

in bright autumn sun. I'm
wrapped in a blanket, a white
knit cap on my head hiding

all but a fringe
of straight black hair.
His lower lip broods.

In today's Cirque du Soleil
when the director stops
rehearsal to ask

Who are you?
what the actor does next
without words—a flip,

a handstand, a trick
on rope—can change the entire
course of the circus.

If somebody had stopped my father
to ask who he was,
would it have made

his mouth less dry
to mime with a flourish
putting pen to paper?

There's a letter he wrote
at twenty courting my mother
in eloquent prose,

my patrimony
though I don't realize it
till the snows thaw this year.

I wish I could tell my father:
May you be not afraid.
May you be a child of five

again, thriving
far from Bucktown's cinders
and broken glass. May you see

within the hardest heart
the spot for love
is soft as a fontanel.

Josie

At first, it's hard to breathe,
dozens of tiny black umbrellas
opening in the lungs, mob scene

crowding the palace for a lynching,
sending a counterfeit rose
to the cheeks. Later,

the dunking under water,
the jitterbug gasp for air.
Consumption was the word

my father used. What did he feel,
as he watched the toothless lion
devour his sister?

He rode bareback from the room.
Enlisted in a war that ended too soon.
Fell for the bite of whiskey

erasing her stillness in the box,
those lids thin as petals
of a morning glory. *Josie.*

With a wish in his voice, facing
the fiery hoop of birthday candles.
That's how he'd say it.

Chicago Morning

A girl in star-print pajamas
is running up the stairs.
It is the daylight called broad

in crime stories.
She reaches the landlord's porch
with its tall thin windows

and a rocking chair
severe as Whistler's mother.
The door to the landlord's flat

is closed. She crouches
behind the chair, shivering
in the summer sun pouring gold

on the red linoleum.
She stays there, huddled
inside her dark wood

like a kid in an air-raid shelter
waiting for the all clear.
No one comes after her

from the flat below. Her father
doesn't need a gun.
He has hands big as a bear's.

Child with Reader

The little girl's learning to read.
The book's about a family
on Pleasant Street, their house

not at all like the basement flat
she lives in, a furnace hulking mid-
kitchen, no tub. In winter

the landlord will interrupt a meal
to shovel coal. He's Russian, proud
of the scar on his forehead

from the revolution. His white
hair, short and stubbly, reminds her
of the dog she teased, poked at

through a gate she thought locked.
His fur stood on end.
He broke free and chased her.

The girl shuts the book, still
troubled by the silent w
in "answer." On Pleasant Street

no one dreams as she did
of a skeleton in top hat and tuxedo.
No one trembles at the light-

fingered dark. She runs to her tree.
The landlord's smoking on his porch.
She knows he is watching.

Childish Things

The blood-red velvet dress
with its willowy waist
and long full skirt

like a bell
couldn't possibly fit
any of her squat

baby dolls, and yet
she took it, convinced
it wouldn't be missed

from that toy Elysium.
Then lied about the theft
to her little friend's

mother. Lied again later
when she said it didn't matter
she was barred forever

from that fairy tale house.
Alone with the empty dress,
its heartbreaking puffs

of Juliet sleeve,
she would hold it
to her chest, consoled

by the give and take of the nap
under her fingertips,
having a dream to touch.

Net

She was swimming for her father, close
to shore. Farther out, lurked weeds
and mud, bottomless and cold.
Doing the back stroke, she turned

over, face in murky water, flipped
again over, in wobbly imitation
of Esther Williams, water-baby
smiling to him

grinning back at her from
the tiny beach at Lake Como,
hands in pockets, the row of rental
rowboats bobbing, lapped by waves,

an outboard motor somewhere
stuttering awake. She wanted him
never to walk away, never to find her
alone, to stay on shore, that far

but present, eyes on her always
loving to make him laugh. The jokes.
There was safety in laughter.
It fooled them both.

The Present

I'd never seen a figure-skate like it,
the heel short and squat, half
the usual height. I sat with one
white shoe on my lap, the other shyly

nestled in its Christmas box,
my pre-teen face a smear of tears,
certain I'd be laughed at by my peers:
square, the brain. Siblings grumbled

ingrate, spoiled brat. Weren't these
better than the hockey skates
I'd learned on, hand-me-downs,
and black? I pouted, sulked. Dick

wouldn't take them back, a deal
from Brown's where he worked.
I can't recall a single skate-
related slight or slur. Years

later I wore them to the rink
in Central Park. After that
I lose track, a mystery where
they ended up, consignment shop

or dump. Dick's life scraped
to a halt before I even thought
to apologize, belatedly grateful
for hours on the ice,

the visceral thrill of racing,
tracing clumsy figure eights
when I wanted to escape
without knowing why or what from.

Quel Dommage

My sister's arms and hands
crippled for life. Contortions

just to lift a coffee cup,
hold a fork. She could not

applaud. I wonder, now she's dead,
if she forgave that stray

bullet of a midwife who yanked
too hard on her head, injured

the cervical spine. Picture
Chicago, late August, the air

humid near the river, rank
with dying fish, the midwife

in a rush from house to street,
clutching her bag, her fee,

saying nothing to alarm my mother,
green farmer's daughter, who wanted

a son, holding her firstborn
like a bridal bouquet.

Specs

I felt bad, failing
his tests, the gray-haired
optometrist in Klaus

Department Store. Suddenly,
in junior year,
I couldn't read the board.

Near-sighted, he said,
while I picked out frames
from a rack, pale blue

harlequins. In a week,
walking home with Mama,
new glasses on my nose,

I stopped to gawk
at the giant clock on top
of the Stewart Warner tower.

It's been there all along,
Mama laughed. With her naked eye,
she could see far.

The clock's solemn face
and black numerals
were visible for miles.

I felt small as the ants
on the sidewalk
running from her shoes.

Heiress

My mother kept it
above her bed,

the tiny portrait
of St. Anthony,

my father's patron saint,
honoring the good

so hard to find in him
alive. Mine

since she died,
it lay for years forgotten

in a drawer, surfaced
in my search for a needle.

What to do
with this reminder

of those two I fear
to see again? I shrink

from their heaven,
ask St. Anthony,

famous for finding things,
where is the love.

The Exchange

Grown loose
as her body thinned,
the gold band rolled

end over end
down a hospital corridor,
crouched and hid.

She complained
to her children.
The ring, never found,

was like skin.
It bore witness,
a widow's medal,

to enduring him.
Bargaining
with the Black Madonna,

she gained two years.
Johnny found her
slumped against a wall.

Nails glossed, a first,
she was buried
with her black leather purse,

two sticks
of Doublemint gum,
a rosary and a poem

her daughter wrote
out of love for who she was
and what it cost.

Position of Strength

I lifted hand to face in self-defense.
She thought I meant to hurt.
My mother sputtered outrage
at my nerve. I hung my head. Could not
explain. Grown, I demonstrate,
to jog her memory, stir up
guilt: "I did *this*. To protect
myself." And do not add
"from you." She's forgotten.
I was twelve. Deprived of oxygen,
her cloudy eyes roam and land
on a space close to my voice.
She sinks into her chair
as if displaced. She would be born
again. And I am still her little girl
lost in Logan Square. Learning
not to move so she can find me.

Thoughts of a Potato-lover

The old woman never learned
to swim. The man she married
could, thrown young

into the river, a quick
study. Her brother died
one week after he nearly

drowned, his arms flailing
like a live oak
in a storm. Her memory's

muddy. She had two daughters
whose soapy heads
she dunked under water.

Sputter. Shudder.
An unforgiving wind rocks
the pane. She's always loved

the sound. Two daughters,
yes. Both could float
like a dead man.

Regrets

Pa scoffs
you're holding them flowers

like a baby.
Good money for the mums,

the white costume.
The bride thinks

what a thing to say
but alters the bouquet

she will toss like salt
over her left shoulder.

In years to come, one
hand to her mouth, afraid

the dead listen,
she quotes with pain

what Pa claimed of her husband:
he's a good man.

It was Ma who grumbled,
banging pots.

Damages

The ax. Felix. Rowdy.
Just a boy. The doll's
head smashed.

Porcelain chips. How
did Lizzie's hand
get in the way? Four

fingers chopped.
Blood-soaked pinafore.
Pa! Pa! No docs

in Robinson. A vet
water-walks, sticks
digits back, wraps

strips of cotton round
and round. A daughter
miracle, Pa floored

as Jairus in the Bible
story: *Talitha Koum.*
White life-long scar

flashing resiliency
when she slices bread.
Felix, old and death-

bed sweating, calls
for her. Lizzie rubs
the scar. Does not come.

In Changing Light

Beside the bed
a torpedo of oxygen.
Children came and went
with big eyes.
My mother didn't cry.
Like Chouchou,
Debussy's daughter,
she kept her tears inside.
We lived so far away
from the farm,
I barely knew her,
my mother's mother.
She adored Lena Horne
in *Stormy Weather*,
and didn't much like
my father. Before
I was born, Daddy
had a dog named King
who protected him
with his teeth.

Anna and Helen

"What difference does it make
Papa chose?" Anna nibbles babka,
back of hand for napkin, the Posnan

aristocrat long stamped out
by the farmer's wife. Helen sniffs,
aligns her fork on the tablecloth,

complains once again, "But you married
for *love!*" Anna huffs, eldest.
"No excuse to be mean! *This*

Victor gives you! Electricity!
Plumbing in the house! You have
a daughter and a son!" Helen twists

a bead of her long coral necklace.
"Please," she whispers, "Anna,
I turn from him in bed." Silenced,

Anna clears, runs water in the sink
until it almost overflows, washes
china frail as Helen's wrists,

and thinks of Ignatz, of waking
with his arm on her breast. Helen
stares at Anna's back, broad and solid

in a faded cotton house dress.
A dove coos loss in the pear tree.
Like a tired swimmer quitting the pool,

she pushes up from the table
with both hands. Morning sunlight
flashes on her solitaire.

Tense

In the Dutchman's drawing
of the pollard trees

the woman holds a rake
over her shoulder,

the man, farther ahead
and smaller,

is surrounded
by his willing sheep.

They plod, backs bent,
through a field

without end, like the ring
in the riddle song.

Do they share a history
of facts and dates

without the salt
of intimacy?

Everything sketched
in inky black

has turned the brown
of dried blood

and muddy waters.
Even the trees

seem on edge,
those two

plodding forward
with their backs to us

as if their language
had no word for good-by.

Dies Illa

It's modern, graveside,
to shield the bereaved,
postpone the final

creak of straps till after
the limos leave. Not so
cremation's nascent

protocol: mourners at the wall
must bear the squeak
of lazy iron fly

crawling up marble, a digger
in a jumpsuit astride
the lift's tiny platform,

in his hands the precious
bronze cigar box
carried like a lunch.

The director calls "it"
John, as if indeed my brother
lived there, poured

in lumps like sugar or salt,
small as Alice post-drink.
He is placed, stuck to rest

in peace, the niche so high
it's hard to read names,
the refrain "What is John?"

like an answer in reverse
playing Jeopardy,
haunting and tormenting.

Teneo

The summer he came back from the war
he took her downtown for a movie
and Chinese. Afterwards, they walked down

Michigan, the wind watering their eyes,
blowing her skirt. In Charmet's,
he splurged on banana splits, a vendor

sold him a rose. It was not a date.
He was her brother celebrating late
her graduation, his coming home

safe, training her what to expect
when a boy asks you out. Now he's dead,
she wonders what she did with it,

the painting on silk. He'd copied her
high school photograph, sent it home
from Japan rolled up like a scroll.

Everyone said it was a good resemblance.
She didn't like the way she looked.
It's here somewhere, hidden in a drawer

for her children to find. The rose,
in her mind, is still alive and red,
as if freshly taken from his hand.

Elegiac

I hold a funeral for the farm.
In my head, like music returning,
the mewing of the blind

kittens, my mother's mother
in a drab cotton house dress
pointing to their nursery,

a crate lined with straw.
She left Posnan and silks
to be a farmer's wife.

I didn't speak her language.
From the pump in the yard
I fill a dented cup; here

is where they drank, the horses
I shied from. I discover
artifacts: a green-black

feather in the coop,
a corncob stripped clean,
light as a hornet's nest.

It hurts to see the beam
the turkey hung from,
waiting for the ax.

Beyond the weathered fence,
row on row of blackberries
ripen, untended.

They taste of sun and rain,
her fortune in a strange land:
baptismal gowns, black arm bands.

Mary, Mary

And this is where they found him in the snow.
At first we thought a hunter's shot a deer.
My husband's gun. My garden does not grow.

A prescient dream the night before: a crow
bugling taps in the pine the barn is near.
And this is where they found him in the snow

in a circle of blood. It's where they'd go,
the boys, to play soldier. It's been a year.
My husband's gun. My garden does not grow.

They kept his casket closed. My heart was slow
to be the loving one, the morning star.
And this is where they found him in the snow.

My brain's a blur. The farm has vertigo.
What kind of mother loves a dead son more?
My husband's gun. My garden does not grow.

Oh sky, how long must I cry out to you?
The dark before the dawn's my hemisphere.
And this is where they found him in the snow.
My husband's gun. My garden does not grow.

Old

I am that leaf spinning nowhere, sere.
I mourn the loss of everything my own.

I loan a frail shoulder to the young,
envy their longer road, cry for more

than happiness at weddings, knowing
what's in store. I want a lying mirror,

arms in bed to hold me when I'm cold.
I am struck by the crushed squirrel,

pigs in trucks peering out through slats.
I light safe electric candles

for my dead, my prayers lame, cracked
as the moon's crust. Each morning,

grateful for breath, another sun,
I cling to the only skin I know.

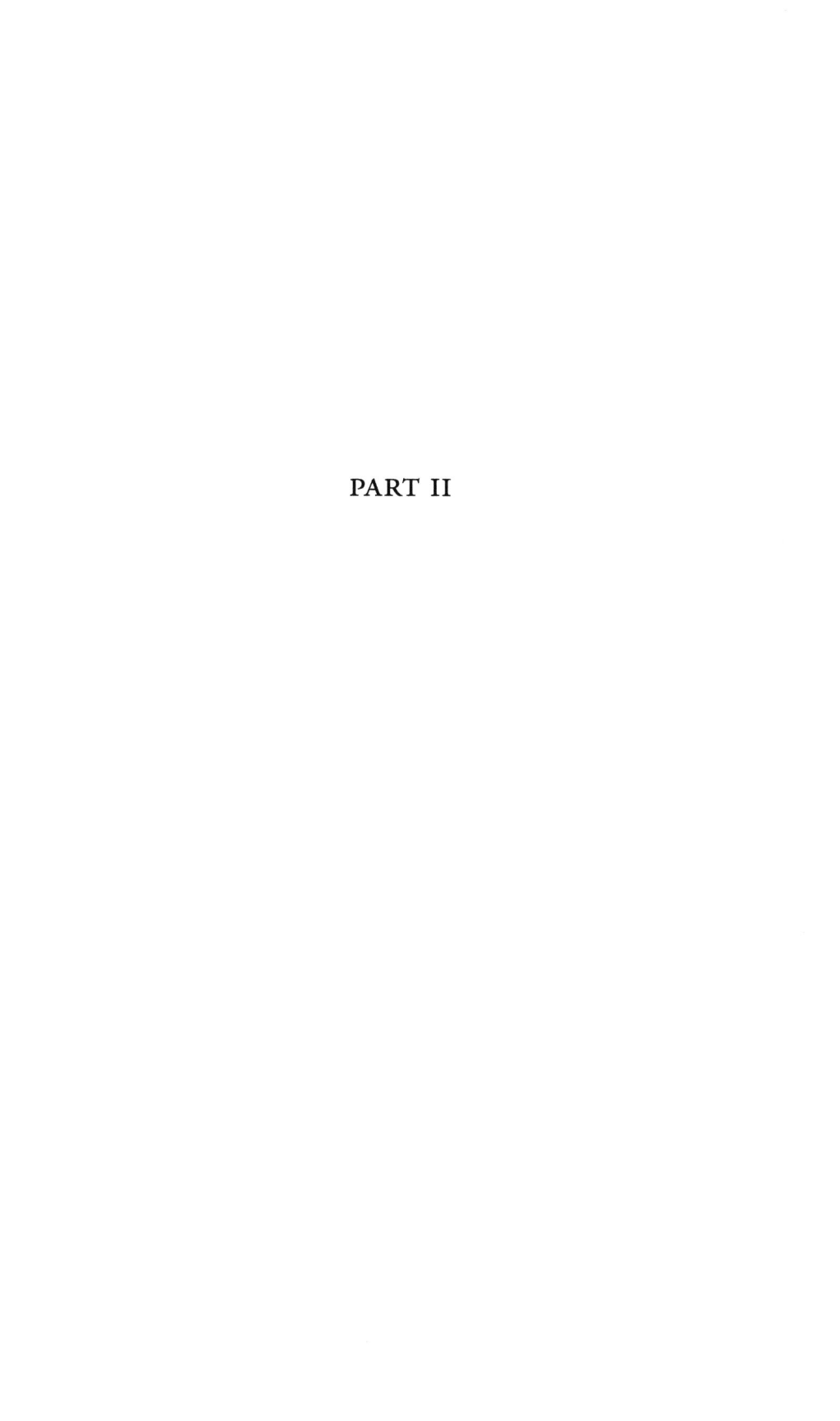

PART II

The Return

I don't recognize her face; it keeps
changing, as if drawn
by a sketch artist keeping up
with my thoughts. Her dark eyes
well up as she says to me
and you've lost a son. I don't ask
how she knows this; osmosis,
clairvoyance, a digital
grapevine. Only then do I recall
hearing news of her untimely
death. Only then do I remember
her name. I don't know what
to make of it, seeing her so
alive. Before bed,
I'd been reading Chekhov
on how things end: a sleepy child
who kills a child, a bishop
stamped out by typhoid
in Holy Week. Was I primed
to receive her? She shines
through the dream
like a lighthouse beam
pointing out the rocks
where ships are broken. Round
and round she goes,
my black Madonna,
telling me this is not the way.

Rachel

This isn't Argentina.

He isn't *disappeared*.

A daredevil,

he has the skin of a pear,

easily bruised.

Is he sleeping in his car?

Has he enough to eat?

I keep looking for his eyes

in the rearview mirror.

Have they been blackened

by a fist?

Tonight there's frost.

I don't know where my son is.

Day 5

A sweater on a chair reaches out
through the dark. I see it
by the light of the street-lamp,
the jabbering moon. It's 4 AM.
I think of Cromwell at the block,
denied the clean stroke, executioner
missing and missing the mark,
the prisoner's shirt dyed red
as a cardinal's hat. I wish
I could change the past, prevent
what is happening now. When
is compassion futile? I sleep,
dream of a boat slipping off
from a pier, stealing into a river,
the oars dipping and lifting me
through the dark, my face half-
hidden by a cloak. I am holding
my son to my breast, resigned,
a dimestore pietà.
I promised him a good life.

Stage IV on the Coma Scale

He throws one skinny leg
over the bed-rail,
searching for the floor

with his foot
before he pulls it back.
It's like a dance routine

he wants to nail
though he can't even walk.
Or a riff on the lines he wrote

found in his backpack:
Can't tell you a dream.
Can't help you with mine.

His eyes don't track.
Is he blind, worn out with waiting
for the right time?

I watch him bite the rail,
the white cotton mitts
flailing in frustration.

What country is he in
without a flag? He stops me
at the border.

Lamentation of Christ: Sold Off to Pay Debts

This is no oasis of peace,
    Mantegna's dead Christ, the body
        foreshortened, the head

enlarged, more like a wounded
    dwarf's, the focus
        on the shrouded genitals:

behold the man. The ribcage looms
    as it must have heaved to breathe
        on the cross, fighting

gravity, the lips stiff and taut
    with suffering unrelieved
        even on the slab,

Mary, John, and Magdalene looking on
    with all the helplessness
        of those who love

and can do nothing. A painting
    Mantegna saved to grace his coffin.
        Something about the model's

mouth, the angle of the head, the chin.
    I'd not expected this resemblance
        to my son. The accident

stole mobility, his mind. Fifteen months
    of cruel, extravagant hope.
        I was sleeping when he died.

Still Life with Timex

At last I am mad enough
to part with the boots,
surly and yellow, the laces cut.

A heavy thud when they land
in the bin. Maybe someone
at the dump will rescue them—

like soldiers in battle
who steal from the dead.
Surely he will walk again.

I'll buy him new.
Unnerving, the way his watch
still runs, the crystal

whole despite the impact,
the second hand rounding
the face in tiny jerks.

In the Meadow

There's a picture of him
in the slideshow:

a boy with bandy legs
hanging from a branch,

on his face a climber's
monkey joy. Taken years ago

when I brought him here
to see the cows, the clouds.

Now I say out loud
I don't know where you are.

A leaf drifts down
from the oak.

Kayakers in the river.
An insect, half grasshopper,

half bee, buzzes the thin
orange marker. Lands,

clings, flies off,
veers back. Again

and again. Deliberate,
persistent

as grief. Look.
A white butterfly.

Isadora
loose in the meadow.

PART III

World on East 84th

Often I hear her singing in 5D,
the svelte soprano with the French
twist. We share a lighter heart

for blonde Jim in 4G. I let him be
Hamlet if he wants, brooding
drama major. One night while he's

starring on my couch, she starts
and stops, begins again,
perfectionist, practicing a lied

in high German. We thrash about
in the dark, our ship going down
to what has to be Mahler.

The furniture tilts, slides, a cut-
glass vase breaks, spilling
the remains of a red red rose.

He casts me off like a shirt.
The fish in its globe swims to me
through dooms of separation.

The Improvisation

The doctor teaches me abandon.
What it must be like
to sky-dive

or race downhill between
a zigzag of birches.
I am his afternoon snack,

his blood-sugar elevator.
Sometimes the doctor plays
Rodrigo for me

over the telephone.
Plucking the dawn
from the strings

of his classical guitar,
he soars like a condor
in his green surgical gown.

I have not yet seen
someone close
flipping helplessly

on the bottom of a boat,
with teeth grown large,
the skin drawn tighter

over bone. Medieval monks
slept in their coffins
to remind themselves

of journey's end.
I have the doctor's eyes
to look in.

Merrily, Merrily

He is an actor who plays doctors
and losers. Gawky
and boyish, the type

old ladies like to feed.
I am not afraid, a good sign.
It's my dream, so I'm in charge

of central casting.
He keeps waving good-by,
a six-foot-two firefly,

and he's there for a reason.
I put him in the light
as if he were a difficult

boss or in-law, for which
there are seminars. Abracadabra
and he's gone, as if Circe

sucked him back into the woods.
The BBC arrives with camera crews.
I tell them I have found

the blue door, through which I row
with infinite dexterity. Where
would I be without these oars

from the Salvation Army, without
the cast of thousands before me
who slept on stones?

Children of Another Century

With you
there are no blindfolds.

Sometimes
I want to cry out:
our ocean is too deep,
these skeins from the heart
too fine
to bear so rich a weight.

But then the torch we light
bisects the dark.

And when we speak,
our words stand eggs on end
to prove the world is round.

And I am Isabella,
crossing beside you.

On a Fragment from Sappho

Just now gold-sandaled dawn
slinks in
like a celebrity

who feels entitled
to the room
and everything in it.

The change from night
to day takes place
imperceptibly

as a belly swells
beginning a child.
Or as love turns slowly

over time
to a wine more sweet
or bitter. Soon

nothing's left
of night's stilettos.
By dawn's yellows,

mirrors come to life
and give back
what they get: a face

fresh with sleep,
the thin or rounded
flesh of an arm,

a sparrow poised
on a shoulder
naughty as Lesbia's.

Again

It's my companion's home town,
bleached by the sun,
robbed of all color and life.
It's so pretty, I lie.

I need to master this
compulsion to please.
The weak spire of a church
pokes the sky: *why why why.*

My mind was elsewhere
when I said it. On green
slopes in a lovely mist.
The west of Ireland

warming a heart that's been
cold too long,
hiding behind the body
of a dead soldier.

Spent

I'm so easily swayed
by the flags you raise,
homage to Keats

evaporates
on my tongue. I hear
only Spanish poets now

with your red soul.
There are no ships
behind your claim

to the river. No gold.
Above the headboard,
farther

than hands can reach,
eternity weighs.
You look down

your classical nose,
turn sideways
to show off your profile,

a Roman coin. Meanwhile,
I wonder
if it's myself

I don't want to find
flip side,
rendered unto Caesar.

Sketch: Fade to Black

Laughing, she leaves the car
to shoot the sign
for Pennsylvania Avenue,

oversized and green,
citified, comical
in rural West Virginia.

Sullen, out of the picture,
her partner kicks
at stones, inspects

the finish
on his baby blue
Monte Carlo. She ends

the roll and winds
her way over, smiling
notice me. A nerve

below his cheek bone
twitches. Jeans tight,
he loosens his belt,

folds his lean frame
into the driver's seat.
She gets in, goes

quiet as the spider
dropping down
on the upholstery.

Steep

All night long
rejoicing
in our bodies

I saw petals
rippling in my mind.
Brilliant, sunlit.

Did I merely wish them
white? (I've seen
petals brown

with shame, Pauline
in what I've done
or failed to do.)

Leaving, bound
for Metro, you cup
your hands to light

a cigarette,
don't look back,
which fails my test

this will last.
My eyes
in the rearview

mirror (there must be
some mistake)
darken, swim

with the carnal
sadness of Latino
virgins. As if

you'd held me
hostage, beneath my chin
a keen stiletto.

White, A Sequel

We laughed when a stranger
blew his horn at us,
flooded your pick-up's cab

with headlights.
I forgot my live-in lover.
You forgot your wife.

But then you stopped
short, swinging your
baseball bat of remorse:

two young sons to hurt.
It was I who struck out,
pleading, "just one night,"

until no motel
was small enough.
I sent a poem, tempting.

You never answered.
Four years later,
a freak accident,

the same pick-up truck
we struggled in
sinking to the bottom

of a pond, did you say
my name or even think it
as water crept up

past handles I'd touched?
When I heard,
I wrote another poem about

us. I called it "White."
For the first snow.
For the color of mourning in China.

Evolution

One false move
ripples across his lifetime,
leaving nothing

untouched: his wives,
his children, this girl
with sloe eyes

who brings him breakfast
in bed, a blood-red rose
slanted in a vase.

He watches himself
butter the bread
as if each grain were pristine

and joined to him.
Is he not a figure
of renewal?

To pull up revenge
like a weed.
But what of the hole

the weed would leave?
The yolk of the egg
tastes like silver.

Bonsai Lovers

Bound to this plot,
to be minimized
like a star
seen from earth,

the telescope
always in reverse,
we press against
the fine wire

holding summer
to its limits,
cutting time
to a function of size.

Confined, we dream
of climbing
Himalayas, of rapture
on a beach.

We are the fall
fashion line, conceived
as an afterthought,
teeth set

for a difficult birth:
the hips too narrow,
the position
breach.

Cumberland

They have followed the canal this far
to Cumberland. His idea.
Inside the Visitor's Center

he's cornered a forest ranger,
they're talking guns. She waits
in the car in the cold. It's

almost dark when he strolls back,
whistling, Nikon on a strap
gently whacking a spot

below his rib cage. He slides
into the driver's seat, rips open
a fresh pack, lights up. Eyes

locked on the road ahead,
he hugs the wheel, left shoulder
inching skyward as the rain

slowly comes. She slips
closer to her door, the air
blue with smoke, cracks

the window. A stream of cold
whistles in. The cows she saw
en route have all gone home.

She cries softly to the slap slap slap
of the wiper blades, thunder
in the west, fading kettle drums.

Unrequited

My knowing all along
the formula
in black marble,

the golden house of God
not a pastorale.
The stage set: Keats

would drown, Teresa
pull out the dart
and throw it back,

catching the angel
off guard,
each candle burnt down

to a nub, hopeless
as my efforts to explain
the altar's sweet smoke

of indifference,
what I saw through,
what I could not believe.

At the Pavilion

Sonatas fill the hall.
The piano roars, a migraine
with perfect pitch.
The cello beats its breast,

mea culpa, incorrigible
masochist. These musicians
are old hands at making
conversation, eyes

behind their heads.
The audience swoons,
ardent scholars of the scale,
insatiable savants. I suffer

the noise, the deaf man's
music, stand outside
the ovations, a lying
derelict sheep. Encores

postpone departure.
I have no taste for them.
It's silence I want, the hole
the knitting holds.

Before the Snow

He's glued to the spot,
the old man in front of me,
a gap of several feet

between his cart
and the checker. I ask
are you in line, and as he turns

I recognize his face,
though it's bloated now
and puffy. He who whined

in our first shower together
the unforgettable
I've got soap in my eyes!

seems smaller, shrunken,
naked without his glasses.
Perhaps I am mistaken.

But no, the well-trained checker
thanks him by name.
He gives no sign he knows me,

a woman of a certain age
bundled up for heavy snow
about to fall. He looks lonely

as Uncle Vanya. Two days later
I'm floored by his letter. Crafty.
Charming as ever. The complete

angler. He hasn't changed
in twenty years, poor bastard.
Nor have I, shredding the cheap

copy paper, certain well-wrought
phrases shining, sticking
hook-like in my head.

Willow

How quickly she forgets the green she wore.
Pouting in yellow, she would break the glass
the water makes, and mourns the years that pass
so rapidly with age. Somehow a door
has closed and left her stranded here to pour
her giant soul into a demitasse.
Those chary clouds begrudge her touch of class.
Beset by shifty genes, they build, and bore.
She, round in a square, unfit, drops her lines,
dysfunctional, confused by nature's tricks
that leave her standing on November's stairs,
the golden girl of myth revived, who pines
for a solution even as she licks
her chains, flaunting her good-for-nothing tears.

Waking Alone on Sunday Morning

The bed warm, the house cold,
the sun bold as Paul

setting out for Rome
and certain death,

I surrender to languor.
The birds have flown south.

A dog barks to be let in.
Each year, hearing

for the first time
the double coo that gave

the bird its name, Wystan Hugh
would note the moment

in his diary, calling it
holy, the return

of the ordinary
knocking him to his knees.

The two-note wonder
fortified,

like two blue clouds
in a child's drawing

of the sky, white
because it doesn't have to be.

PART IV

Tremor

The blonde doll from the thrift shop
falls from her perch. It's not

reindeer landing on the roof. Two
porcelain Fu dogs lie face down

on the carpet, as if worshiping
a god underground. The santos

of Anthony looks up at me
with coal-black eyes

that can read a soul. I'm grateful
nothing broke. My legs

wobble, cowards as I walk.
Outdoors, I wave to neighbors

I've never spoken to before.
Together in our fear,

we are geological agnostics:
earthquakes don't happen here.

I see again my mother's lips in death,
as if her final say

were slashed in clay by a sculptor.
The radio wails:

the Washington Monument's cracked,
the National Cathedral.

Tombs

It's the morning after still another death
on the cross. The sky cooperates
with a limousine shade of gray

and there's a curious muting of birdsong.
The entire window to my soul is a ripe olive,
verging on midnight or a soft coal,

severe as the eyes in Byzantine icons.
What's to be done when memory serves a god
stooping from his niche

with a shudder of wings? When grandeur
sucks at the loading dock?
One can polish despair to a high gloss

slick as a crow's wing. One can focus
on messages stored in the body—
a flimsy fortress.

One can dare to ask out loud
what happened then and turn more shades
of black than Frans Hals' forty.

The Cardboard Shirt

Convinced the wooden buttons
aren't the final touch,
you take the shirt

outdoors, hose it down, soak it
through, so that it dries
rough as tree bark. This,

despite your teacher's advice:
Stop! Too much fiddling
may *destroy* a work of art!

The shirt wins a prize, over years
slowly fades—a rip, a tear,
the damp. You find it when,

to keep your children safe,
you seal off one room
with duct tape, store food

and bottled water, map
your escape. You're pleased
the sleeves thrust out

suggest a small boy's arms
stuffed in a snowsuit,
that first walk to school

alone, a mother looking on.
You run your fingers over work
you knew how to complete,

certain what was best,
and see Isaac looking up
into his father's eyes.

Black Messengers

Ghulam's not a lord losing his eyes
in Lear, but a farmer in Helmand Province
where poppy's king. Three men show up

in the night, stifle his cries
with a rifle butt. His wife and children
watch as a thug inserts a knife,

breaks the windows to his soul. They
take nothing from the house, leave
behind, flickering in each brain,

a slide show for all seasons. Was this
a random act of violence? A plan
of the Taliban? No one claims

it was us. The provincial mouthpiece
rues the tragedy. Ghulam learns to walk
with a stick, plant by touch.

In Padua: St. Anthony's Tomb

Feeling trapped here
by crutches and canes,
snapshots of the smiling

cured, I think of the bones
within, the crook
of humerus, radius, and ulna

that held, legend says,
the infant Christ.
Superstition, my dead

friend George
would have said
of this shrine, this crowd

of believers
expecting a miracle,
among them a young girl

chemo-thin, slumped
in a wheelchair.
Supplicants swarm the tomb,

press both hands
to the stone.
Not knowing

what's to become of it,
my body takes over.
I, too, lean into the stone.

Rowhouse Angel

Wrapped up in vines,
she stands out in the light

of a thousand-watt bulb.
Who would want an angel

of such proportions
in their own back yard?

She reins in giant wings.
Will assume no other pose

even if the trumpet sounds.
Perhaps she was chosen

not to guard a lawn
rife with brown spots

and fading yellow roses,
but for the stone itself,

a stab at permanence.
Maybe she said *touch me.*

*I am as solid and real
as you think I am.*

I Underestimate What She Meant to Him

I tip the spade. The orange
clump of Virginia dirt lands
with a thud. Scores more to come
before this gentle stoning

of the coffin ends. Even the sun
looks wronged, as if stuck
in the angry stage of grief.
My red-faced friend curses

in the car over a wrong turn,
a missed exit. His tears dark
and public, he can't forgive her
leaving. He's like the small boy

running to tell his mother
the cat's got a bird in its mouth.
He is falling. Scrapes his knee.
He is happy to feel the burning.

Hopkins Room, University College, Dublin

Everything waits: black coat and clergyman's
    black biretta, coiled ivory rosary
        on the mantel. Back soon,

they seem to say, like the sun
    promising to return to Dublin,
        the sky mouse-gray with rain.

He didn't die here on the white iron bed,
    was taken, ailing, to a lower floor.
        Better care there, more light.

Soon stars, cold as doubt. *To see,*
    but not to see by, he warned
        of their spark, swimming

through the dark to the sanctuary.
    Dying, he said it twice: *I am so happy*,
        the poet of carrion comfort

come to terms with lines unseen,
    Glasnevin's unmarked grave, the arctic
        silence of his speckled Lord.

Eutychus Propped on a Windowsill
Listens to Paul

Drowsy, you close
your eyes in sleep, topple
from your perch

and fall
three flights down
into an alley.

You cannot see the torches
flood the stairs
or feel Paul's weight

pressed lightly as a sheet
on your flesh. You cannot
hear him singing

from the dark road.
Paul is
pin and ointment, out

of the body, a flower
on the fracture, praising
for the grass,

the sleepy town of Troas.
He breathes into your skin
a pinkness, soothing

the fearful: *His life
is in him still.
By morning he'll be whole.*

Luke weaves your story
into Acts, homely,
lacking the show-stopping

power of Lazarus walking.
Ours to imagine you
waking, stretching, talking,

recalling nothing
of the fall from a windowsill,
the weight of Paul.

Sara's Song

The child I cannot have
is yours.
We welcome it.
We see it like a city
we have always wanted to see.
We look into its eyes
transparent as a sailor's wife
listening
for his footstep on the stair.
Those eyes make us one
turn of the heart.
We burn the icehouse
where God used to live.
It's as if we'd set finches
loose from their cages,
we have so much light to protect.

Unlike Anybody Else in the World

The cow dips into Trollope,
the perfect escape
from thoughts of the slaughterhouse,
the children whose whereabouts
are unknown. He is cool
as the water under a tree in summer,
delightful even when he interrupts
the plot (damn the suspense!)
to elaborate on a folly, warn
of things to come. She turns to him
on mornings when there's no sun.
He brightens her stall, the straw.
She can lose herself in his cathedrals,
in drawing rooms where men stand
with their backs to the fire
and women with brains and grit,
strong-willed and principled,
can be counted on for more
than serving tea. (The cow identifies
with Madame Max Goesler.) And lauds
his genial grays: no one in Trollope
totally qualifies for villain
or saint. It could be said he loves them
most for their faults, their Pauline
"doing what I would not." Such merciful
understanding. A blessing then
to roam his imaginary county,
to linger in the shadow of his towers.

Poem on a Line from a Sufi Prayer

He is reading in bed, his wife asleep.
High winds are tearing up the sky.
In the dark, before he sleeps,

unseen, he weeps. He has no one
to be brave for. A tree,
in another part of the city,

uproots, destroys a house,
but the couple inside escapes
without physical injury. Their story

news on the radio next morning
as he drives through town to work
reeling in bits of last night's dream:

he's alone in a boat, grounded
on the back of a turtle streaked
with blood. His father killed it,

expects him to devour its flesh.
Mark me like the tulip with thine own
streaks, the Sufi mystic pleads.

The boat becomes a star
looking down on him reading in bed.
His wife believes he is fearless.

Shenandoah Scene

Burnt sienna legs
lie folded over
torsos and heads.
Three dead does,

wine-dark blood
sprinkled on coats.
Was this a black rite,
skinhead origami?

The trees ad lib,
exhaust their repertoire
of leafless hymns.
The river's voice

is locked in ice,
like someone new to grief.
Eyes picked clean
speak loud as guns

of the dispatch,
the hack and slash,
the insane Feng Shui
on the river bank.

For Edward Thomas

Easter Monday, Germans
on the run, the Brits

whoop and dance in mud
and snow, celebrate

the rout. A pause
in the shooting, Thomas

leaves the dugout,
is about to fill his pipe

when a stray shell
whizzes past his post,

nails his heart. He falls,
unmarked, on each page

of the war diary
tucked in his pocket

a bizarre arc of creases
from the shock wave.

Preserved in the poet's
crabbed hand, a line he wrote

just days before: *And no more
singing for the bird.*

Iconic Photo: Lee Miller in Munich, April, 1945

On a table beside his tub a small statue
  of a kneeling woman, nude, right arm
    draped over her head. Was it always

on display, or has it been transported
  for effect? Like the photograph of Hitler
    propped on the tub's edge. A picture

within a picture of Miller in the water,
  washcloth to her shoulder as Scherman clicks,
    records a face that betrays no disgust

her body's touching what Hitler's body touched.
  Muddy boots on the floor. Clothing
    loosely tossed on a backless chair

suggests she acted on impulse, driven
  by images from Dachau: mouths agape,
    staring eyes locked on air. Cables

Vogue: I IMPLORE YOU TO BELIEVE THIS IS TRUE.
  Shocking, what she bore witness to, where
    her boots have been. The tub's

enormous, more like a hard white sarcophagus,
  its porcelain and chrome ordinary
    as sin, as Eichmann.

Musings

Say Keats had lived a decade more, a score,
and stayed in Rome because he loved the wine
of old buildings, the drama in a pine
at the Farnese, the hot sun's allure
more than Fanny's soggy England. Say he
then sought out Leopardi for his sublime
poverty of style, the silvery chime
of the *Canti* drenched in melancholy.
Flinched at the sight of a hunchback who wrote
like an angel. Thought better of his own
physique, short but straight, not a single bone
tortured as that frail "S" in a waistcoat.
Toasted broom, lively on a precipice,
fragrant desert flower thwarting darkness.

Concerto

eyes closed his rapture
no secret
he draws the bow
the soul of wood
responds to
the soul of Elgar

the cellist
head back
ecstatic in stiff
white collar
makes public love
to his instrument

to die this way
submissive
as a wolf in defeat
he takes us where
we would not go
alone

deep inside a birth
the pure wave
come to cleanse
flooding
through his hands
like Ganges water

At the Museum of the Resistance

The reflection of my face
on the glass
blocks out the yellow star.
I have to look harder.

Who wore it last?
If I broke the glass,
I could hold the star
in my hands. Would I

feel the terror?
I was a child in America
having nightmares
when the shoah was born.

The guard folds his arms
across his chest
like Il Duce. I nod to him
as if to say

I'm harmless. Nevertheless,
I feel uneasy, like a fish
swimming away
with a hook in its mouth.

A Catastrophe of Violins

I look through a window
at an old year.

Surely someone
should retrieve these instruments

for the poor. But no,
they hang here, articulate

as a mountain of shoes,
of hair, witnesses

in the box, swearing
to tell the world

nothing but the truth.
The room is as long

and wide as I imagined it.
I am a cantor

hungry for music
where there is none.

The Secret Historian

I knew he'd left the university for skin art—
    wolves and butterflies, names in hearts—
        his own tattoo shop on South State Street,

a career change he didn't mention in his letter
    advising me to be the kind of writer
        Sigrid Undset was. Shocking to think

of him in bed with withered Bosie, lovers
    by the hundreds skin to skin, my proper
        teacher who looked like Clifton Webb

keeping a stud file, diaries documenting trysts
    and orgies, his taste for rough sex, a life
        style become the stuff of Kinsey. Why

so many lays? Why bare his neck to little foxes
    set on spoiling him? When doctors said
        his cancer of the testicle was a twin,

a malabsorbed embryo, Sam, shattered, wondered
    if he had but half a soul. He died alone,
        mourning his dog, unintelligible

in the end as anyone under the skin.
    I prefer to remember him, pencil mustache
        quivering and prim, class about to begin,

gathering up his things, announcing
    before he stepped down from the podium:
        Ladies and gentlemen, it is spring.

Christt to Kazantzakis

When you shall not see me more
than this flash of diminishing sand

go into the wilderness of your own accord
practicing the divine

pianissimo.
Like the stork graceless on land

take off in beauty equal to the hawk.
When the time comes to begin again

make angels in the sand,
spare the reed shaken in the wind

as if none of this were true
(although we seem to know who we are)

and hope for prevailing stars to
fall like an augury.

Capital

Where? Where?
Gull cries on the bridge.

The Potomac out there,
hidden in fog as planes

on instrument
head into National.

Ramp signs barely visible.
Pity the stranger

counting exits to DC.
Tractor trailers

and town cars snake
towards the landmark

dome. Faith-testing,
this human tangle

on wheels, coming
closer to the city

unknowable
as the blank rune.

We let our children go
into this fog.

Farther Out

She meets herself coming and going
through windows and doors streaked
with red paint, play-blood,

counterfeit to fool the angel. Toy
bills and coins. Hard truths
to whistle Dixie to in the dark.

No dibs on happiness, she turns
for solace to the gulls, pelicans,
the cathedral of water swarming

with particles she cannot see
any more than she can see God.
Like Crane pulling off his robe

to jump ship and meet his left-
handed destiny, she walks out,
wise in the work of immersion.

Admiral to Isabella

here are my credentials
to be your Columbus
navigate waters

exotic and pure
guiding eyes and fingers
a potpourri of bones

to gain in concert
a realm of sunlight
nothing broken

could you be
my gnostic angel
my gold in a purse

velvet wings descending
in a haze
do birds know this too

I say to heaven
O Seigneur
I must learn your language

flora and fauna
double helix on Plato's wall
double rainbows Isabella

Acknowledgments

Artemis: "Josie;" *Arts & Letters*: "The Return," "Before the Snow;" *Azuria*: "Tombs," "Patrimony;" *Birmingham Poetry Review*: "The Cardboard Shirt," "Position of Strength;" *Bloodstone Review*: "At the Pavilion;" *Chautauqua*: "Steep," "Unrequited;" *Cimarron Review*: "Heiress," "Spent," "Teneo;" *Cumberland River Review*: "Rowhouse Angel;" *District Lines Summer 2014 Anthology*: "Tremor;" *Ekphrasis*: "Tense;" *Ellipsis*: "Child with Reader;" *FIELD*: "Chicago Morning," "Merrily, Merrily," "A Catastrophe of Violins," "Capital;" *Gargoyle*: "Childish Things," "The Present," "On a Fragment from Sappho;" *Gulf Coast*: "*Lamentation of Christ*: Sold Off to Pay Debts;" *Hippocrates Prize Anthology*: "Stage IV on the Coma Scale;" *Iron Horse Literary Review*: "Regret;" *Litrag*: "The Improvisation;" *Montserrat Review*: "Concerto;" *Mudfish*: "In Changing Light," "Waking Alone on Sunday Morning;" *North American Review*: "Evolution;" *Ocean State Review*: "Rachel;" *Pacifica Literary Review*: "Bonsai Lovers;" *Parabola*: "Hopkins Room, University College, Dublin;" *Poet Lore*: "Anna and Helen;" *Potomac Review*: "Old," "Willow;" *Salamander*: "Mary, Mary;" *Sou'wester*: "Day 5;" *Southern Humanities Review*: "At the Museum of the Resistance;" *Southword*: "World on East 84th," "White, A Sequel," "In the Meadow;" *Sow's Ear*: "Net," "Farther Out;" *Tar River Poetry*: "Still Life with Timex;" *The Texas Review*: "Quel Dommage;" *The Alembic*: "Specs," "The Exchange," "Thoughts of a Potato Lover," "Children of Another Century," "Again," "In Padua: St. Anthony's Tomb," "Admiral to Isabella;" *The Blueshift Journal*: "Poem on a Line from a Sufi Prayer;" *The Journal*: "Damages;" *The MacGuffin*: "Shenandoah Scene," "The Secret Historian;" *The Natural Bridge*: "Stains: The Wrong House," "Sketch: Fade to Black;" *The Yale Review*: "Musings," "Unlike Anybody Else in the World," "For Edward Thomas;" *Tiferet*: "Eutychus Propped on a Windowsill Listens to Paul," "Sara's Song;" *Underneath (anthology)*: "Iconic Photo: Lee Miller in Munich, 1945;" *Virginia Quarterly Review*: "Dies Illa;" *Women Arts Quarterly Journal*: "Black Messengers," "I Underestimate What She Meant to Him;" *Xanadu*: "Christ to Kazantzakis."

"Elegiac" originally appeared in *The Southern Review* and also was featured on *Poetry Daily*. "Iconic Photo: Lee Miller in Munich, 1945" won the 2015

University of Canberra Vice-Chancellor's International Poetry Prize. "Still Life with Timex," "Rachel," and "Tense" were nominated for a Pushcart Prize.

Thanks to the editors of journals who have published individual poems, and to Dave Parsons who selected *Heiress* as a runner-up in the X. J. Kennedy Poetry competition. Kudos to the editorial and production staff at Texas Review Press for designing the book and cover art. I am grateful to those who have supported and encouraged my work over the years, especially Sue Lawless, Jeanne Sorrentino, David Kuebrich, Betsy Beyler, Nita Congress, Sue Hoffmeyer, Dana Green, Saideh Pakravan, Barri Armitage, Jane Frakes, Rebecca Foust, Elizabeth Stoessl, Susan Bianconi, Sandra Barnett, Tex Vathing, Sharon Ewing, Robert Murawski, and Sheila Murawski. And finally, thanks to my parents and my beautiful sons—Christopher, Jesse, and Alex—and their families.

CPSIA information can be obtained
at www.ICGtesting.com
Printed in the USA
BVHW03s0333220818
525120BV00002B/32/P

POETRY

Murawski is a master of consummate poetic craft, as comfortable in handling the rigors of formal poetry as she is the subtle demands of distinguished free verse. The poems of this remarkable collection sparkle with biblical and musical allusion, and timely references to a litany of literary and historical personages: from Chekhov to Cromwell; Hamlet to Mahler; and Sappho to Keats.

"A brave poet undaunted by the darker realities of experience, Murawski probes, with haunting insight and emotional honesty, the somber hues of a home bereft of love; an unwanted child; a sister crippled at birth; childhood and relationship abuse; and the insatiable yearning lurking at the core of universal human existence."

—LARRY D. THOMAS, 2008 Texas Poet Laureate

"Here is the work of a master wordsmith, bringing the reader poignant stories, memories, and the closest observations of the human experience. . . .Though these are highly personal poems, they are woven in deeply emotive responses to literature: Hopkins, Sappho, Chekhov, Crane, and many others. These stabbing lines will find permanence in many, minds."

—DAVE PARSONS, 2011 Texas Poet Laureate and author of *Reaching For Longer Water*

ELISABETH MURAWSKI is the author of *Zorba's Daughter*, which won the May Swenson Poetry Award, *Moon and Mercury*, and two chapbooks. Her work has been published in *The Yale Review*, *The Southern Review*, and *FIELD* among others. A native of Chicago, she currently lives in Alexandria, Virginia.

★texas review press
Huntsville • Texas
www.texasreviewpress.org

ISBN 978-1-68003-168-3